All Around Texas

Regions and Resources

Mary Dodson Wade

Happy summer 2014!

Love,
Grammy & ...

Heinemann Library
Chicago, Illinois

D1211166

© 2013 Heinemann Library
An imprint of Capstone Global Library, LLC
Chicago, Illinois

Customer Service 888-454-2279

Visit our website at **www.heinemannlibrary.com**

Designed by Kimberly R. Miracle and Betsy Wernert
Photo Research by Tracy Cummins
Printed and bound in China by Leo Paper Group Ltd

13
10 9 8 7 6 5 4 3

New edition ISBNs: 978-1-4329-1150-8 (hardcover)
                   978-1-4329-1157-7 (paperback)

The Library of Congress has cataloged the first edition as follows:
Wade, Mary Dodson.
  All around Texas : regions and resources / Mary Dodson Wade.
      v. cm. -- (Heinemann state studies)
Includes bibliographical references and index.
Contents: An introduction to Texas -- The coastal plains -- North
central plains -- Great plains -- Mountains and basins -- Map of Texas.
  ISBN 1-4034-0686-3 -- ISBN 1-4034-2694-5
1. Texas--Geography--Juvenile literature.
2. Regionalism--Texas--Juvenile literature. 3. Texas--Description and
travel--Juvenile literature. [1. Texas--Geography.
2. Regionalism--Texas.] I. Title. II. Series.
  F386.8.W33 2003
  917.64--dc21
                        2003009548

Acknowledgments
The author and publishers are grateful to the following for permission to reproduce copyright material:

Cover photograph reproduced with permission of ©Getty Images/Bruce Dale

p. 4 Robert Hashimoto/Heinemann Library; **pp. 7, 28** Eleanor S. Morris; **p. 14** George H. Huey/Corbis; **p. 16** David R. Frazier Photolibrary; **p. 17** VanHart/Shutterstock **p. 18** Richard Cummins/Corbis; **pp. 19, 23b** Corbis; **p. 20** Grant Heilman/Index Stock Imagery, Inc.; **p. 23t** Brian Miller/Bruce Coleman, Inc.; **p. 24** Greg Smith/Corbis SABA; **p. 25t** Charles O'Rear/Corbis; **p. 25b** Bryan-College Station Eagle, Butch Ireland/AP Photo; **p. 27** Dana Hoff/Corbis; **pp. 29, 38** Bob Daemmrich Photo, Inc.; **p. 31** Carolyn Brown/Getty Images; **p. 32** Bob Mahoney/The Image Works; **p. 33** Robert & Linda Mitchell; **p. 34** James P. Rowan; **p. 37** Buddy Mays; **p. 39t** Billy McDonald Jr./Bruce Coleman Inc.; **p. 39b** Marcelo Wain/iStockphoto; **p. 41t** David Muench/Corbis; **p. 41b** Digital Vision/Getty Images; **p. 42** Joseph Sohm/ChromoSohm Inc./Corbis **p. 43** Buddy Mays/Corbis; **p. 44** Joel Salcido/Bob Daemmrich Photo, Inc.

Every effort has been made to contact copyright holders of any material reproduced in this book. Any omissions will be rectified in subsequent printings if notice is given to the publisher.

Contents

Some words are shown in bold, **like this**. You can find out what they mean by looking in the glossary.

An Introduction to Texas

Anyone who tries to describe Texas after visiting only one part of the state would not provide a complete picture. Texas is huge and **diverse**. It is second only to Alaska in area. Its borders stretch 800 miles (1,288 kilometers) from east to west and the same distance from north to south. It covers 267,277 square miles (693,539 square kilometers). Water makes up 6,784 square miles (17,571 square kilometers) of Texas.

Forests, deserts, plains, and mountains come together in Texas. The state's four geographic regions are called the Coastal Plains, Central Plains, Great Plains, and Mountains and **Basins**. Each region has **unique** land formations, its own **climate**, and various **natural resources**.

This part of the San Antonio Valley is in the Coastal Plains region of Texas. The region is known for its rich soil.

Land Regions of Texas

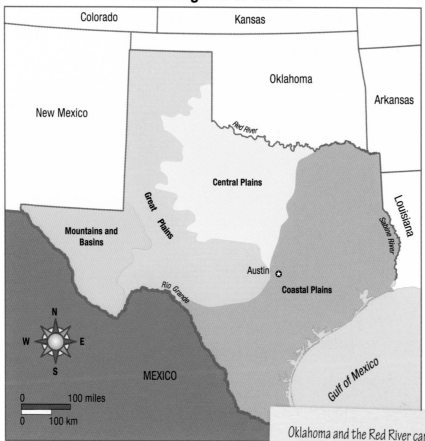

Oklahoma and the Red River carve away the north side of Texas. New Mexico makes a huge notch on the west. The Rio Grande forms a boundary with Mexico. The Gulf of Mexico scoops out the southeast coast. On the east, the Sabine River separates the state from Louisiana. At its northeast corner, Texas is bordered by Arkansas.

Land

Much of the land in Texas was formed when huge plates of the earth's crust pushed together. About 600 million years ago, this movement helped to form granite, a kind of rock. Granite rocks are the oldest rocks in Texas. They are found in the Llano (LAN–oh) Uplift in the middle of the state. During the next 250 million years after the rocks formed, shallow seas washed across north, central, and west Texas.

Glaciers never touched Texas. But as glaciers melted and reformed elsewhere, the seas around Texas rose or fell by 300 to 450 feet (91 to 137 meters). About 3,000 years ago, the Gulf of Mexico reached the level at which it sits today.

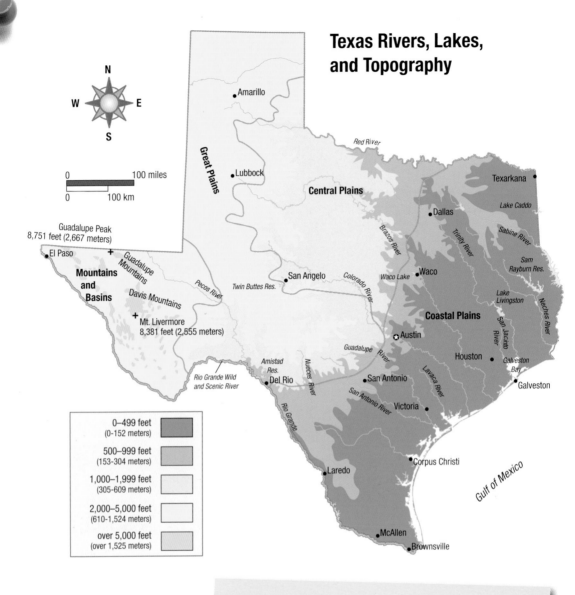

Texas Rivers, Lakes, and Topography

N
W E
S

0 — 100 miles
0 — 100 km

Amarillo

Red River

Texarkana

Great Plains

Lubbock

Central Plains

Lake Caddo

Dallas

Sabine River

Brazos River

Trinity River

Sam Rayburn Res.

Guadalupe Peak
8,751 feet (2,667 meters)

El Paso

Guadalupe Mountains

Mountains and Basins

Davis Mountains

Pecos River

Twin Buttes Res.

San Angelo

Colorado River

Waco Lake

Waco

Lake Livingston

Neches River

Coastal Plains

San Jacinto River

Mt. Livermore
8,381 feet (2,555 meters)

Guadalupe River

Austin

Houston

Galveston Bay

Amistad Res.

Nueces River

Rio Grande Wild and Scenic River

Del Rio

San Antonio

Lavaca River

Galveston

San Antonio River

Victoria

Rio Grande

0–499 feet
(0-152 meters)

500–999 feet
(153-304 meters)

1,000–1,999 feet
(305-609 meters)

2,000–5,000 feet
(610-1,524 meters)

over 5,000 feet
(over 1,525 meters)

Laredo

Corpus Christi

Gulf of Mexico

McAllen

Brownsville

Texas's highest mountains are found in the Mountains and Basins region in western Texas. Dams along rivers provide flood control and form **artificial** lakes that provide recreation and drinking water.

Water

Texas has 13 major rivers and more than 11,000 named bodies of water. Most of the rivers start in Texas. The rivers all drain into the Gulf of Mexico. The 600-mile- (966-kilometer-) long Colorado is the longest river entirely inside the state. *Colorado* is Spanish for "red." The Brazos river system is over 1,000 miles (1,600 kilometers) long. It travels through many of Texas's geographic regions. The Rio Grande begins in Colorado. *Rio Grande* means "large river." Water from the Rio Grande is used for **irrigation** and **recreation**. The part between Big Bend and Amistad **Reservoir** is designated as the Rio Grande Wild and **Scenic** River.

The shortest river in Texas is the Comal. This 2.5 mile- (4 kilometer-) long river empties into the Guadalupe River. Its waters once provided power for the **industry** of New Braunfels. Much of the property along the banks is now parkland.

Texas has more than 6,700 lakes and reservoirs. All but one are artificial, or human-made. Caddo Lake in eastern Texas is the state's only natural lake, but even that lake has been enlarged by a dam. River authorities for each major river provide flood control. Dams create artificial lakes called reservoirs. Reservoirs provide recreational areas. They are also sources for drinking water and irrigation. Under Texas law, all freshwater belongs to the state. Users of this water must have a permit.

Groundwater comes from **aquifers**. Aquifers lie under 80 percent of the state. More than half the water pumped from them is used to irrigate crops. Texas has 9 major aquifers and 20 minor ones. The rapid growth of cities and increased crop irrigation has lowered the water level in Texas aquifers. Arguments between city governments and farmers of Texas competing for the same water have often wound up in court. Aquifer authorities work with river authorities and water **conservation** districts to protect water sources. Lake water seeps through the soil to refill aquifers. But the Ogallala Aquifer in the Great Plains region must depend on rain in an area that gets little rainfall. There is concern that this aquifer will dry up.

Climate

The climate of Texas depends on the region. The lower Rio Grande in the Coastal Plains region is the warmest part of the state year-round. The coldest part of Texas is the northwest part of the Panhandle in the Great Plains.

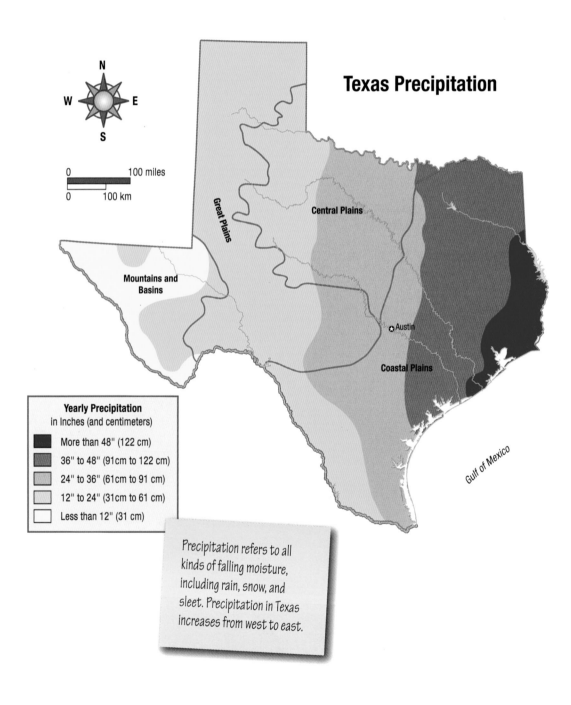

Texas Precipitation

Yearly Precipitation
in Inches (and centimeters)

- More than 48" (122 cm)
- 36" to 48" (91cm to 122 cm)
- 24" to 36" (61cm to 91 cm)
- 12" to 24" (31cm to 61 cm)
- Less than 12" (31 cm)

Precipitation refers to all kinds of falling moisture, including rain, snow, and sleet. Precipitation in Texas increases from west to east.

Texas has a warm, wet climate along the Gulf of Mexico. Winds from the Gulf help to keep temperatures more livable in both the summer and winter. Central and northeast Texas are **temperate**, and can be hot in the summer and cold in the winter. It is cool and dry in west Texas. Northwest Texas can sometimes have cold winters.

Texas sometimes gets heavy rain coming from the northwest. Tornadoes are a threat during warm-weather months across much of the state. The central and southern parts of Texas rarely see any snow, though they sometimes get freezing rain. However, the High Plains in the western part of the Panhandle get about 2 feet (61 centimeters) of snow a year.

Blue Northers

"Northers" appear on the horizon as gray-blue clouds. A cold wind from the north drops the temperature 15 or more degrees Fahrenheit almost instantly. Temperatures may continue to drop slowly for several hours.

Natural Resources

The most valuable natural resources for Texas's economy are its **petroleum** and natural gas. Texas is known for its huge petroleum deposits, which are some of the largest in the world. The largest deposits of petroleum and natural gas are found in west-central Texas, near Midland and Odessa. Texas has other valuable mineral resources that are mined. These include sulfur, salt, limestone, clay, gypsum, and lignite, to name a few.

Texas also has rich soils and grasslands. The state has over 1,000 different types of soil. They range from heavy clay, to rich **loam**, to fine sand. About 78 percent of the state is good pastureland and farmland. The variety of soils allows Texas farmers to grow many kinds of crops. Cotton is the state's leading crop. Texas produces more cotton than any other state. Most Texas cotton is grown in the Coastal Plains and Great Plains regions. Corn, **grain sorghum**, hay, rice, and wheat are also important crops for Texas's economy.

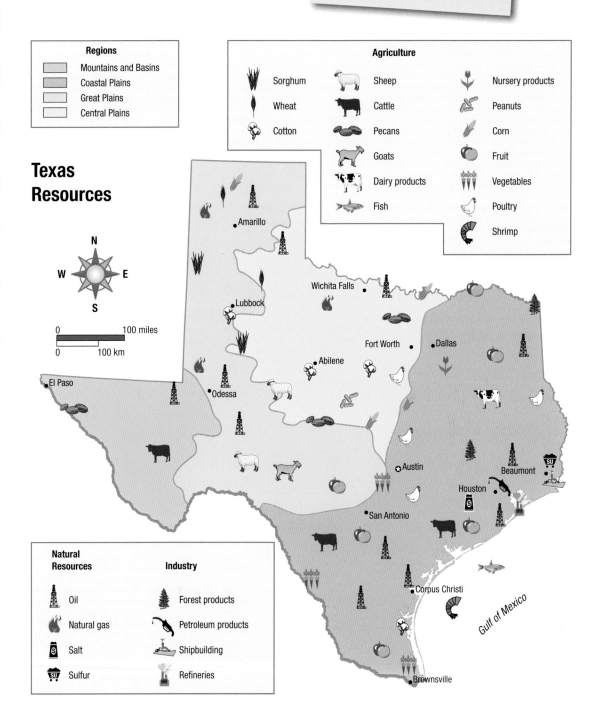

The state of Texas has a variety of resources, industries, and products in each of its geographic regions.

Regions

- Mountains and Basins
- Coastal Plains
- Great Plains
- Central Plains

Agriculture

- Sorghum
- Wheat
- Cotton
- Sheep
- Cattle
- Pecans
- Goats
- Dairy products
- Fish
- Nursery products
- Peanuts
- Corn
- Fruit
- Vegetables
- Poultry
- Shrimp

Texas Resources

N
W   E
S

0   100 miles
0   100 km

Amarillo

Wichita Falls

Lubbock

Fort Worth   Dallas

Abilene

El Paso

Odessa

Austin   Beaumont

Houston

San Antonio

Corpus Christi

Gulf of Mexico

Brownsville

Natural Resources

- Oil
- Natural gas
- Salt
- Sulfur

Industry

- Forest products
- Petroleum products
- Shipbuilding
- Refineries

10

Using Resources

At one time, most Texans were farmers. In 2006 there were about 230,000 farms in Texas. That's twice as many as in any other state. Agribusiness is one of the main sources of income in Texas. Agribusiness is more than growing and harvesting crops. It also includes processing, transporting, and marketing farm products. Farm products include both food and nonfood products, such as cotton.

Workers in Texas manufacturing plants produce products relating to the oil industry, such as chemical and petroleum products. They also make industrial machinery, electrical equipment, and transportation equipment. **High-tech** products, such as computers and electronic parts for cellular phones, are a new industry in Texas. Many of the products made in Texas are **exported**. Texas provides about 14.5 percent of all United States exports. About 35 percent of the **goods** produced in Texas go to Mexico.

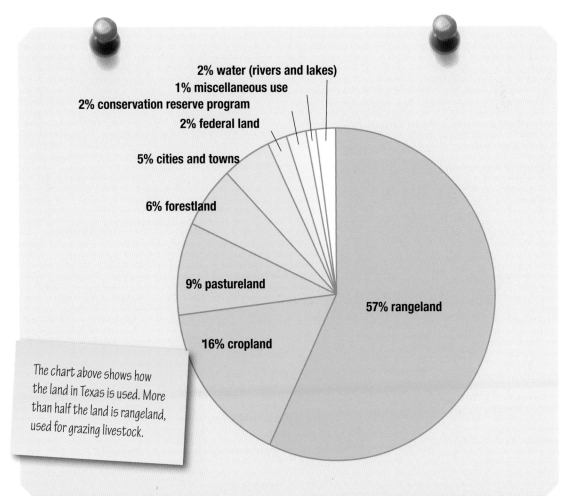

- 2% water (rivers and lakes)
- 1% miscellaneous use
- 2% conservation reserve program
- 2% federal land
- 5% cities and towns
- 6% forestland
- 9% pastureland
- 16% cropland
- 57% rangeland

The chart above shows how the land in Texas is used. More than half the land is rangeland, used for grazing livestock.

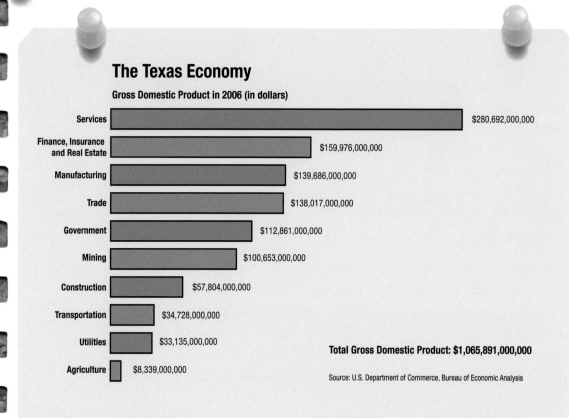

The Texas Economy

Gross Domestic Product in 2006 (in dollars)

Services	$280,692,000,000
Finance, Insurance and Real Estate	$159,976,000,000
Manufacturing	$139,686,000,000
Trade	$138,017,000,000
Government	$112,861,000,000
Mining	$100,653,000,000
Construction	$57,804,000,000
Transportation	$34,728,000,000
Utilities	$33,135,000,000
Agriculture	$8,339,000,000

Total Gross Domestic Product: $1,065,891,000,000

Source: U.S. Department of Commerce, Bureau of Economic Analysis

Texas has one of the largest economies in the world. The total value of items produced is called the **Gross Domestic Product** (GDP). In 2006 the state's GDP was over one trillion dollars! That is larger than the Gross National Product (GNP) of many countries.

Oil and gas make up ten percent of Texas's economy. Until the 1980s, the amount was 25 percent. But after a sharp drop in oil prices, other industries developed. Construction is a major industry in Texas today, as cities rebuild and **suburbs** expand. Almost 22 million people live in the state's four main regions, with 84 percent of all Texans living in **urban** areas. The construction industry answers the need for more homes and offices. The construction industry includes the workers who do the construction and the workers who produce the products the builders use.

The largest number of Texans, however, work in the service industries. Most of them live in urban centers. They provide services for other people by working in offices, hospitals, churches, hotels, restaurants, banks, theaters, and stores. They sell cars, insurance, and property. They also transport goods. Or, they may be part of the police or fire department or some branch of government.

Coastal Plains

The largest region of Texas is the Coastal Plains. It covers the eastern third of the state. The land changes from flat to rolling hills as it extends north and west from the Gulf of Mexico to the Red River.

About 220 million years ago, the North American continent split apart from Europe and Africa, forming the Gulf of Mexico. Seawater left salt deposits, which eventually formed salt domes. Salt domes in the Texas coastal plain trapped oil and natural gas in the rocks that surrounded them.

Coastal Plains Subregions

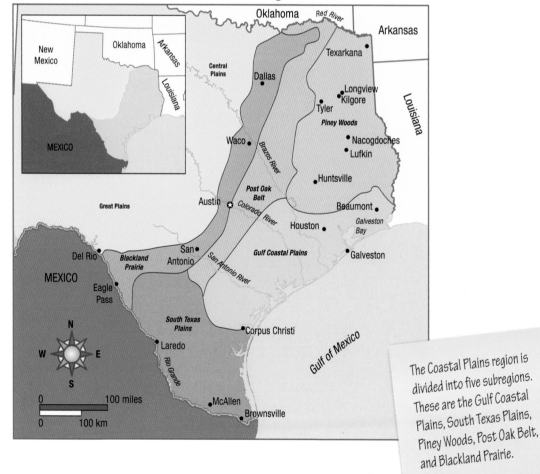

The Coastal Plains region is divided into five subregions. These are the Gulf Coastal Plains, South Texas Plains, Piney Woods, Post Oak Belt, and Blackland Prairie.

13

During this period, the land moved again, forming the Ouachita (WASH–e–taw) Mountains in east Texas. Seas still covered west Texas. Limestone **reefs** around the edge of the seas formed pockets that became part of Texas's oil **reservoir**. Eventually, westward-flowing rivers **eroded** the Ouachita Mountains. Today, the eroded Ouachita Mountains lie under east Texas.

Shallow seas again covered much of the state 140 million years ago. During this time dinosaurs, giant **mollusks**, and flying reptiles lived in Texas. About 75 million years ago, deeper water covered much of Texas. River **deltas** formed sandstone in east Texas. These rocks became reservoirs for the east Texas oil field.

Padre Island has over 130 miles (209 kilometers) of beaches. Padre Island National Seashore is the largest undeveloped seashore in the continental United States.

Gulf Coastal Plains

The southeast part of Texas follows the Gulf of Mexico, from Orange down to Brownsville. **Barrier islands** and **peninsulas** form threads of land just off the coast. The largest island is Padre Island. It extends the length of the south Texas coast. Most of the island is a national seashore that has been protected and left in a natural state.

The Gulf Coastal Plains extend from the eastern state line to just past the city of Corpus Christi. A person driving the whole length of the plain would never see a hill. The clay and **loam** soil drains poorly. Away from the coast, farmers raise rice, grain, corn, cotton, and hay. Cattle graze on plentiful grass.

Ten rivers enter the Gulf of Mexico in this region. The Brazos and Colorado flow directly into the Gulf. The others enter bays first. Many shallow bays and **marshes** line the coasts. About half the marshes are freshwater.

Beaches on the Gulf Coastal Plains attract tourists. Gulf breezes blow from the southeast. They pick up moisture and cause high humidity. Palm trees and tropical flowers thrive. Grass stays green throughout the year, and freezes rarely occur.

The high humidity in the Gulf Coastal Plains sometimes brings violent weather. Hurricanes and tropical storms can cause loss of life and property. The media warns of approaching danger. Signs mark safe roads for people to use while fleeing storms.

Europeans Land in Texas

The location of Texas on the coast of the Gulf of Mexico meant that it was visited by early explorers and ships. Shipwrecked Spaniards landed on Galveston Island in November 1528. After eight years, Álvar Núñez Cabeza de Vaca and three companions reached Mexico City. Cabeza de Vaca, whose name means "head of a cow," wrote the first book about Texas.

The Gulf Coastal Plains are the center of the nation's **petrochemical industry**. Along the coast from Beaumont to Corpus Christi, **refineries** and chemical plants light up the night sky. They are located on the coast so that oceangoing ships can easily move their products to other parts of the world. Many products are moved on **barges** along the Intracoastal Waterway. The Intracoastal Waterway runs from Brownsville, Texas, to the east coast of the United States. It provides calm water for the tugboats to steer barges.

There are some large cities in the Gulf Coastal Plains, including Houston, which is the largest city in Texas. Houston traces its beginnings to 1835, when brothers Augustus and John Allen sold lots there. The Allens claimed that ships from New York City would visit Houston. Eighty years later, the Houston Ship Channel, a 50-mile (80.5-kilometer) channel, was **dredged** through Galveston Bay and up Buffalo **Bayou**. The Houston Ship Channel is one of the world's leading centers for **distributing** energy and chemical products. Today, the port of Houston is 25 miles (40 kilometers) long. In total tonnage of **goods**, it ranks second in the United States. Houston is the fourth largest city in the United States.

Refineries and Petrochemical Plants

Refinery towers capture **petroleum** liquids at different levels. Ones that evaporate easily, like cleaning fluid, come off at the top. Lower down, gasoline is caught, and still lower, diesel fuel. The sludge at the bottom of the tower is used to make asphalt for paving roads.

Some of the separated material is broken down even farther. This is sent to petrochemical plants that produce material used to make plastics, cosmetics, paint, ink, drugs, pesticides, fertilizers, and explosives.

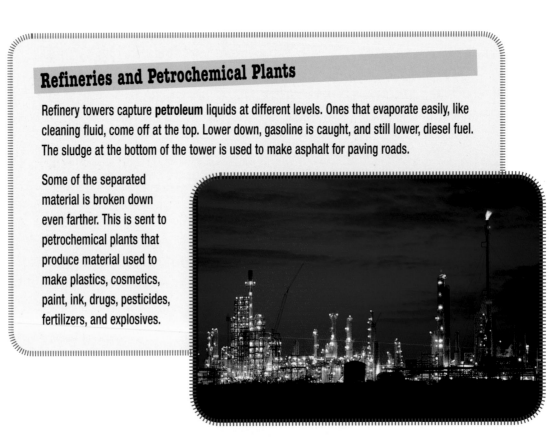

Over 2 million people live within Houston's city limits. The Greater Houston area is more than eight times the size of the state of Rhode Island.

Houston has its own natural air-conditioning system. Most of the streets are like a grid, running north-south and east-west. But the original part of the city has streets on a southwest-northeast angle, running the same direction as the coastline. Gail Borden, who founded the Borden Milk Company, laid the streets out this way with the help of his brother. They wanted the city to catch the cool sea breezes. These breezes help, but Houston remains hot and humid during the summer.

Today, more than 200 companies are based in Houston. Many of the companies, including Halliburton and Conoco-Phillips, are related to petroleum. Continental Airlines also has its headquarters in Houston. KUHF, the first public radio station, broadcasts from the University of Houston.

The world's largest medical complex is at the Texas Medical Center in Houston. The first heart bypass operation and the first **artificial** heart transplant were performed there. Cancer research at M.D. Anderson Hospital draws patients from all over the world.

Houston Control

In 1969 astronaut Neil Armstrong spoke from the moon saying, "Houston, the Eagle has landed." A year later, Apollo 13 commander James Lovell sent an alarming message from space: "Houston, we have a problem." The "Houston" the astronauts spoke to is the control center for the National Aeronautic and Space Administration (NASA) called the Johnson Space Center. It is located in Clear Lake City, 20 miles (32 kilometers) south of Houston. Some 15,000 engineers, scientists, and astronauts work and train at the Johnson Space Center.

Beaumont, another Gulf Coastal Plains city, has shipbuilding facilities and rice mills. But it is best known for opening the modern **petroleum industry**. A well in the nearby Spindletop salt dome blew in on January 10, 1901, resulting in the start of major oil companies such as Texaco and Gulf, which are now part of Chevron.

Galveston, **county seat** of Galveston County, was once called the "Wall Street of the Southwest." It rivaled New York City as a financial center near the end of the 1800s. Much of the city's fortune came from cotton. After a hurricane in 1900 killed 6,000 people, Galveston built a 17-foot- (5-meter-) high seawall from sand dredged from the Gulf of Mexico for protection. Galveston is now a tourist town. Its ten-day Mardi Gras celebration each February brings between 300,000 and 500,000 visitors. Those visitors spend money, boosting the city's economy.

The Galveston hurricane of September 1900 wiped the city away. In terms of the loss of human life, it was the worst natural disaster in American history.

Galveston News and the Texas Almanac

The *Galveston News* is the oldest continuously operating business in Texas. It began with one page in 1842. Fifteen years later, the *News* published a little ten-cent pamphlet listing facts about Texas. This grew into the nearly 700-page *Texas Almanac*, published every year.

Corpus Christi, to the south of Galveston, has many refineries. Tourists flock to the seawall or pass through the city on their way to Padre Island. The Museum of Science and History has exact replicas of Christopher Columbus's three ships of 1492. They were built by Spain in 1992 to celebrate the 500th anniversary of the European discovery of America.

These are Santa Gertrudis cattle. The Santa Gertrudis breed of cattle was developed between 1910 and 1940 at the King Ranch in south Texas.

South Texas Plains

The South Texas Plains fill the area west of Corpus Christi and south to the Rio Grande. Bays cut into the sandy coastline. Few towns exist between Corpus Christi and Brownsville. King Ranch occupies part or all of four counties. This is the largest ranch in the continental United States, with about 60,000 head of cattle and smaller interests in oil and tourism.

Areas away from the coast receive less than 25 inches (63.5 centimeters) of rain each year. Thick cactus and thorny shrubs give the area the name Brush Country. The very southern tip of Texas is called The Valley. Citrus crops and many vegetables grow in the mild **climate** and rich soil. Crystal City is a leading producer of spinach and even has a statue of the cartoon character Popeye.

In the South Texas Plains, Texas cities on the Texas-Mexico border along the Rio Grande benefit from trade between the United States and Mexico. Some factories in the United States ship manufactured parts to Mexico, where Mexican workers in factories called *maquiladoras* assemble the parts into finished products, such as washing machines. The finished products then come to the United States.

Texas Border Crossing Cities

United States City	City in Mexico
El Paso	Ciudad Juarez (see–yu–DAD WHAR–az)
Presidio (pre–SIHD–ee–oh)	Ojinaga (oh–he–NAH–gah)
Del Rio	Ciudad Acuña (a–KUN–yah)
Eagle Pass	Piedras Negras (pe–A–drus NAY–grus)
Laredo (luh–RA–doh)	Nuevo Laredo (nyoo–A–voh luh–RA–doh)
McAllen	Reynosa (ra–NO–sah)
Brownsville	Matamoros (mah–tah–MOR–ohs)

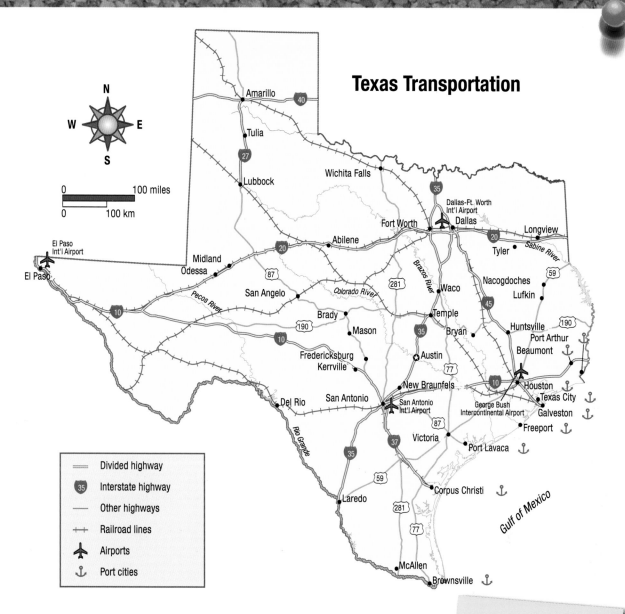

Texas Transportation

Legend:
- Divided highway
- 35 Interstate highway
- Other highways
- +++ Railroad lines
- ✈ Airports
- ⚓ Port cities

It is less expensive to make the products in Mexico because Mexican workers are paid less, so the products are often more affordable for American buyers, and the United States businesses make a higher profit. There is disagreement, however, over whether or not this practice actually benefits U.S. citizens.

Laredo, 200 miles (322 kilometers) up the Rio Grande, is the starting point for Interstate 35 and U.S. Highway 59. Traffic between the U.S. and Mexico has become so heavy at this point that plans have been made for U.S. Highway 59 to be enlarged to become Interstate 69.

Brownsville is a gateway to Mexico and an international port. Seafood processing, electronics, and automotive assembly provide an income for people living there.

Texas has about 300,000 miles (483,000 kilometers) of roads, highways, and streets. It also has many important ports along the Gulf of Mexico.

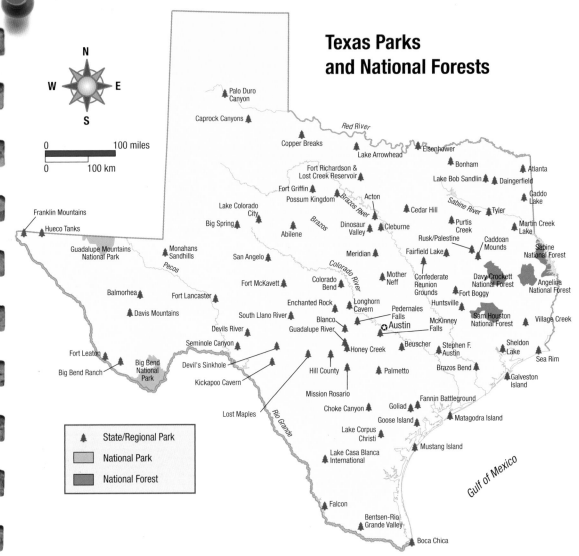

Texas Parks and National Forests

State/Regional Park
National Park
National Forest

The Piney Woods

As its name indicates, the Piney Woods is filled with trees. Thick forests of pine and hardwood cover the area. All of the state's national forests—Sabine, Angelina, Davy Crockett, and Sam Houston—are in this area.

Texas's national forests are all located in the Piney Woods. However, wooded areas and state parks are found throughout Texas.

Piney Woods starts at the Louisiana border about 25 miles (40 kilometers) from the Gulf Coast. It runs north to the Oklahoma border and extends westward for 75 to 125 miles (121 to 201 kilometers). It is often called Deep East Texas. The Piney Woods receives up to 55 inches (140 centimeters) of rain a year, which is more rain than anywhere else in the state. Winters are mild, but freezes occur. Farmers raise poultry and beef and dairy cattle, which graze on the plentiful grass. Fruits and vegetables grow well in the **loam** soil. In recent years, Cherokee County has been the state's leading producer of nursery plants and flowers.

The Big Thicket National Preserve is located where the Piney Woods meets the Gulf Coastal Plains. Cacti, ferns, orchids, beech, pine, oak, and cypress trees are found in the tangled growth and swamps.

Oil is another eastern Texas resource. The first Texas oil well was drilled in Nacogdoches (nak–uh–DO–chiz) County in 1866. Then, in 1930, C. M. (Dad) Joiner found the huge eastern Texas oil field in Rusk County. Northeast Texas employs most people in the state's oil and gas **industry**.

Downtown Kilgore once had so many oil wells that the **derricks** almost touched each other. The East Texas Oil Museum is located there.

Texarkana (tex–ar–KAN–uh), a city half in Texas and half in Arkansas, is a center for distributing agricultural products and lumber. Major highways and interstates pass through this city. Nearby Longview, Kilgore, Nacogdoches, and Lufkin produce lumber, oil, and wood products. Diboll (DI-bawl), just outside Lufkin, is headquarters for Temple-Inland Forest Products Corporation. Huntsville is home to the headquarters of the Texas Department of Corrections.

These workers are loading freshly cut pine lumber onto a truck, near Conroe, Texas. Close to 2 billion board feet (610 million board meters) of lumber are produced in Texas each year.

Post Oak Belt

The Post Oak Belt is an area mostly made up of hardwoods west of the Piney Woods. It cuts a wide path down the center of the Coastal Plains. It runs from the Red River to San Antonio. A variety of soils makes the area good for farming and livestock grazing. The climate is **temperate**. Crops include cotton, corn, watermelon, peanuts, and pecans.

The Post Oak Belt is not just woodlands. This long stretch of farm fields is in the Post Oak Belt.

No large cities are located in the Post Oak Belt. Tyler, the largest town, is actually located between the Post Oak Belt and Piney Woods and is known as the Rose Capital of the Nation. It has a famous rose garden and a rose festival every year.

College Station is the home of Texas A&M University (TAMU). The school opened in 1876, as an all-male military school. It was created as an agricultural and mechanical (A&M) college. The A&M in the name is just symbolic now. The University has a veterinary school and a strong engineering department. The George Bush Presidential Library and Museum is on the **campus**.

This is the Texas A&M University Band playing at a football game. Over 40,000 students attend the university.

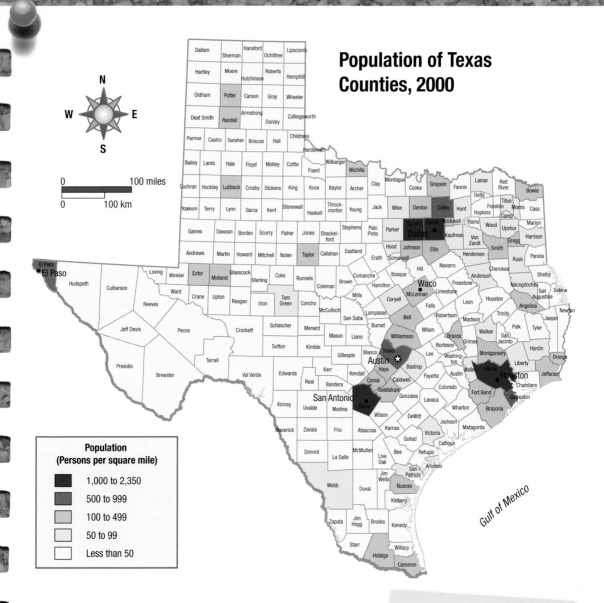

Population of Texas Counties, 2000

Population (Persons per square mile)
- 1,000 to 2,350
- 500 to 999
- 100 to 499
- 50 to 99
- Less than 50

Blackland Prairie

The Blackland Prairie extends from the Red River to south of San Antonio. It is narrow at the southern end and broadens out at the Red River. The soil is loam and black clay. When the black clay dries out, it forms deep cracks. Homeowners often water around their houses to prevent foundation damage.

This map shows the number of people per square mile in all the counties of Texas. The cities of Dallas, Waco, Austin, and San Antonio boost the population of the Blackland Prairie region.

The upward movement of the **tectonic plates** helped to push up the central part of Texas. The uplifted part split from the Coastal Plains along **fault lines**. The Balcones Escarpment formed where the two parts broke apart. The escarpment is clearly visible in Austin.

This is the Dallas skyline. The State Fair of Texas is held in Dallas each fall and attracts about 3 million visitors. That makes it the largest yearly fair held in the United States.

The Blackland Prairie is excellent farmland with a good growing season and 30 to 40 inches (76 to 102 centimeters) of rainfall a year. It was the major cotton producing area of the state until large farms were developed in west Texas.

The Blackland Prairie area contains the largest concentration of people in the state. The four cities of Dallas, Waco, Austin, and San Antonio are located up to 100 miles (161 kilometers) apart. Dallas is the state's second largest city. The city is known as a center for culture and fashion. Buyers come to Dallas to select items to sell in their stores.

Dallas is also a banking and communications center. A number of the largest firms in the United States have headquarters in the city or its **suburbs**. Southwest Airlines is based in Dallas. Exxon Mobil's headquarters are in Irving, where the Dallas Cowboys play football. Texas Instruments in Dallas developed the first handheld calculators and continues **high-tech** research today.

Waco, on the banks of the Brazos River, is a farming, manufacturing, and university town. The Dr. Pepper Company, one of the nation's largest soft drink companies, began here with a soda fountain drink in 1885. Baylor University in Waco is the second-oldest **institution** of higher education in the state.

The Western White House

George W. Bush has a ranch 20 miles (32 kilometers) west of Waco in Crawford, Texas. It became known as the Western White House early in his presidency. He spent time there on holidays, still carrying out his presidential duties.

Austin Music Scene

Austin is proud to call itself "Live Music Capital of the World." More than 100 places have live music playing every night, including country, rock, blues, and reggae. "Austin City Limits," a public broadcasting show featuring musicians, originated here.

Austin, on the Colorado River, has been the state capital of Texas since 1839. The huge pink granite capitol building sits on 46 acres (19 hectares). The main campus of the University of Texas (UT) is in Austin. The school was founded in 1839. It had 52,000 students in 2002, which was the largest student body at any university in the country. The Lyndon B. Johnson presidential library is located on the University of Texas campus.

Many telemarketing companies, which sell goods or services by telephone, are located in Austin. Dell Computer Corporation is in Round Rock, about 20 miles (32 kilometers) north of Austin. Michael Dell founded the company while he was a student at the University of Texas.

Boats carry visitors down the San Antonio River, passing colorful restaurants along the Riverwalk. Tourism is San Antonio's second largest industry.

These troops are carrying out military exercises at Fort Sam Houston in San Antonio. The fort supports all of the National Guard and Army Reserve units in Texas.

The third largest city in Texas is San Antonio. It began as a **mission** in 1718. The Alamo was the mission chapel. People from the Canary Islands, off the coast of Spain, arrived in 1731 and started the city. San Antonio has remained a major city in Texas since then. It is a popular city for conventions, or large business meetings. Tourists from around the world come to see the Alamo. They stroll the Riverwalk with its restaurants, shops, and hotels. Boats carry passengers along the San Antonio River. Tourism brings 4 billion dollars into the San Antonio economy each year. It also provides jobs for about 80,000 people.

San Antonio uses the Edwards **Aquifer** as its water supply. It is one of the largest cities in the world that gets all its water from an underground source.

Many military bases are located in San Antonio. Fort Sam Houston is the one of the oldest continuously operating military bases in the nation. Brooke Army Medical Center is the nation's top-ranked burn center and a research center for **bioterrorism**.

Central Plains

The Central Plains is a large, somewhat square area west and north of the Coastal Plains. It is higher and drier than areas to the east of it. Three subregions make up the Central Plains. They are Cross Timbers, Grand Prairie, and Rolling Plains.

Central Plains Subregions

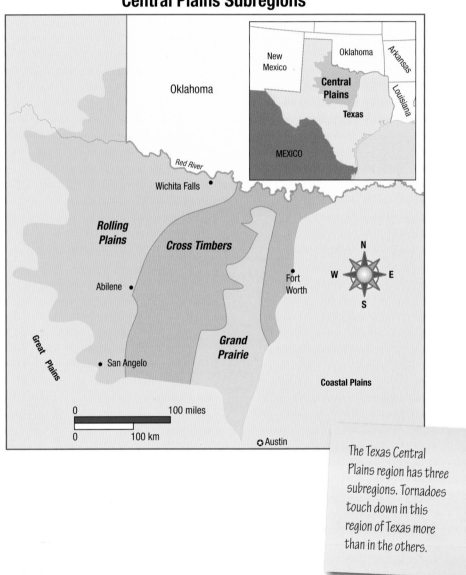

The Texas Central Plains region has three subregions. Tornadoes touch down in this region of Texas more than in the others.

Cross Timbers

Cross Timbers is the name of a wooded area of oak, hickory, and pecan trees. It starts at the Red River in the north. The Eastern Cross Timbers is a narrow strip extending 150 miles (241 kilometers) south from the river. The Grand Prairie area separates the Eastern and Western Cross Timbers.

Farmers in the Cross Timbers grow peanuts, fruits, vegetables, and hay. Texas actually ranks second in the United States in peanut production. Comanche County in the Western Cross Timbers is one of the top five peanut producing counties in Texas. The Western Cross Timbers is much larger than the Eastern Cross Timbers, but fewer people live there. Much of the income of the Western Cross Timbers comes from cattle and oil. The rodeo and cowboy **traditions** of Texas are strong in the Cross Timbers region.

Fort Worth is located in the Eastern Cross Timbers. It is a business and manufacturing center. American Airlines is based at the Dallas-Fort Worth (DFW) airport. Lockheed Martin in Fort Worth makes F-16 fighter planes for the United States Air Force at a site that has made airplanes for 60 years.

The Dallas-Fort Worth airport creates about 11 billion dollars for the north Texas economy each year. In 2006 over 60 million passengers flew into or out of DFW airport.

Grand Prairie

The Grand Prairie is an area of rolling hills with shallow, rocky soil. The land rises to 1,700 feet (518 meters). **Mesquite** and tall grasses make this a good ranching area.

One of the largest army bases in the world is located in the Grand Prairie, about one hundred miles south and a little west of Fort Worth. Fort Hood Military Reservation is home of the U.S. Army's Third Armored Division. It is the largest armored post in the United States. Unlike some military bases, Fort Hood troops leave immediately when a national crisis occurs.

This is a U.S. Army training exercise at Fort Hood. Soldiers from Fort Hood were some of the first to fight in Afghanistan in 2001 and Iraq in 2003.

Rolling Plains

The Rolling Plains extend west from the Western Cross Timbers to the Caprock **Escarpment**. Land just below the Caprock is 2,000 feet (610 meters) high. Flat-topped hills and canyons line the western part of the Rolling Plains. Rainfall is about 30 inches (76 centimeters) in the eastern part of the area and 20 inches (51 centimeters) in the western part each year. The western part is generally too dry for farming. Summers are hot, and winters are cold.

Many large ranches are located in the Rolling Plains. Cattle, sheep, and goats feed on short grasses. Texas has led the United States in the production of cotton for more than 100 years. In 2005 the value of cotton produced in Texas was over 2 billion dollars. The farms that grow most of the cotton in Texas are now in the Rolling Plains region.

This machine is stripping cotton in the Texas plains. Cotton is the state's leading crop, and Texas produces more than any other state.

Wichita Falls, on the border with Oklahoma, is an oil and cattle trade center. San Angelo, in the southern part of the Rolling Plains region, has sheep and goats. It also manufactures medical **goods** and denim jeans, and is a center for **distributing** goods.

Abilene started as a railroad shipping center for cattle. During World War II, Dyess Air Force Base was an important part of the economy there. In 1981 Abilene celebrated its **centennial** by drilling a demonstration oil well, which actually struck oil.

Texas Tornadoes

Tornadoes occur all through the middle section of the United States. Because of its size and location, Texas has more tornadoes than any other state. More people are injured or killed by tornadoes in Texas each year than in any other state. The cost of damages caused by tornadoes in Texas each year is also higher than in any other state. There is an average of more than 100 tornadoes each year in Texas, with 10 deaths and over 100 injuries. The average cost of damages each year is over 40 million dollars. In Texas, tornadoes are most likely to occur along and south of the Red River between Lubbock and Dallas. They are least likely to occur, but do occasionally, in the Mountains and **Basins** region, also known as Trans-Pecos.

Great Plains

The Great Plains region covers other states in addition to Texas. This large geographic region extends down the middle of North America from Canada, through the United States, and into Mexico. The Great Plains in Texas has three sections, which are the High Plains, the Edwards **Plateau**, and the Llano **Basin**.

Palo Duro Canyon

Palo Duro means "hard wood" in Spanish. The name refers to the trees and shrubs found in the canyon. Yucca and prickly pear cactus grow there, too. American Indians used the high walls as a shield against the cold during fierce winters. Food, firewood, and water were plentiful in the canyon. Cattle rancher Charles Goodnight chose the canyon for his ranch for these reasons.

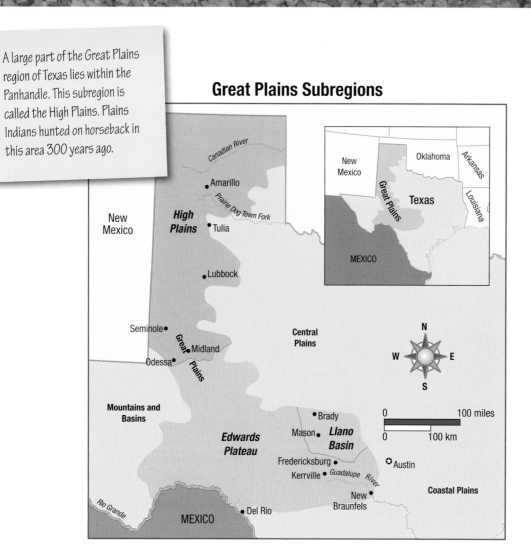

Great Plains Subregions

The High Plains

The High Plains covers most of the Panhandle of Texas. The flat, treeless plain has well-drained clay and **loam** soil. Weather extremes occur in this area. Texas's record low temperature of −23°Fahrenheit (−31°Celsius) occurred in Tulia in 1899 and in Seminole in 1933.

The Canadian River cuts across the Panhandle north of Amarillo. South of Amarillo, the main **tributary** of the Red River, called the Prairie Dog Town Fork, cut a deep **gorge** that formed Palo Duro (PAL–oh DYOOR– oh) Canyon.

In the United States, Palo Duro Canyon is second in size only to the Grand Canyon. It is 60 miles (97 kilometers) long and about 6 miles (9.7 kilometers) wide. Canyon walls plunge nearly 800 feet (244 meters) to the canyon floor. In Palo Duro State Park, the walls form a backdrop for an outdoor summer musical highlighting the history of the area.

Playas are another interesting feature of the flat plains landscape. *Playa* is the Spanish word for "beach." About 19,000 of these perfectly-round, sunken places dot the High Plains. They were probably scooped out by swirling winds long ago. There is no beach, but the playas fill with water when it rains. Hard clay soil holds the water there. Although the Ogallala **Aquifer** lies underneath the High Plains, very little water seeps down into it. The surface water attracts many **migrating** birds on their way across North America. Playas dry up when the water evaporates.

Wealthiest County

The television series *Dallas* created an image of oil-rich Texans living in big cities. The 2000 **census** listed Sherman County in the High Plains as the wealthiest county in the state. The average income of the 3,000 people living in the county was almost twice that of people living in most of the other Texas counties. Resources that help those residents earn their income are oil, natural gas, cattle, and wheat.

The Ogallala Aquifer is the largest aquifer in North America. It extends from South Dakota in the north to the Caprock in Texas, which separates the High Plains and Central Plains. Almost all of the water that Texas draws from the Ogallala Aquifer is used to **irrigate** crops on the High Plains. A plan to pump water out of the Ogallala Aquifer to sell to cities has caused much concern. Some people are worried that the water will be used up more quickly than the aquifer can naturally refill itself.

The High Plains extends 350 miles (563 kilometers) south from the top of the Panhandle. Cattle ranching, farming, and oil are important sources of income for the region. Most of the crops are irrigated from the Ogallala Aquifer. The land north of Lubbock produces wheat and **grain sorghum** and is the state's leading producer of corn. Most of Texas's corn is grown in the Panhandle and is used as feed for livestock. The area south of Lubbock leads in the production of cotton, which is Texas's leading crop.

The very southern section of the High Plains is the location of the huge Permian Basin oil field. Midland and Odessa, at the southern end of the High Plains, are linked by the oil and natural gas production of the Permian Basin.

Amarillo (am–uh–RILL–oh) is the largest city in the High Plains region. It began as a railroad town for shipping cattle. Today, Amarillo is a wheat-growing area. It is also the meeting point for several major highways. The famous Route 66, the first cross-country highway in the United States, once ran through Amarillo. At one time, Amarillo had the largest source of **helium** in the world, but the helium is now gone.

Lubbock, about 120 miles (193 kilometers) south of Amarillo, began as a ranching center. The Ranching Heritage Museum preserves houses and barns from famous Texas ranches. Lubbock is a cotton trade center today. It has the world's largest cottonseed processing plant. Manufacturing in Lubbock includes fire-protection equipment, clothing, and food containers. The main **campus** of Texas Tech University is also located in Lubbock.

This working oil well near Midland pumps oil from deep in the earth. The Permian Basin oil field of Texas produces about 312 million barrels of oil a year.

Edwards Plateau

The Edwards Plateau lies south of the Central Plains, between the Colorado and Pecos Rivers. The Balcones **Escarpment** forms the southern and eastern edges of the region. This part of the state rises up to 3,000 feet (914 meters).

The Edwards Plateau averages 20 to 31 inches (51 to 79 centimeters) of rainfall a year. This supports small oak, **mesquite**, and pecan trees, as well as grasses. Soil is thin, with limestone **outcroppings**. Cattle and sheep thrive in the region. The Edwards Plateau is the center of the nation's wool trade. It has the largest concentration of sheep and goats in the country. This area is the nation's leading Angora goat producing region. Angora goats produce **mohair**, which is used to make fabric and clothing. The Edwards Plateau also has more white-tailed deer than any other place in the United States.

Most goat ranching in Texas is of Angora goats, which produce mohair. Most goat ranches are on the Edwards Plateau, but there are also some in other parts of Texas.

Tourists come to New Braunfels for inner tube rafting on the Guadalupe River and to see Sister M. I. Hummel's famous figurines and paintings of children. Luckenbach was made famous by country singers Willie Nelson and Waylon Jennings. Kerrville has many summer camps along the Guadalupe River. The Cowboy Artists of America Museum is also located in Kerrville. Del Rio is a border town along the Rio Grande. It is a gateway to the Amistad **Reservoir**.

Enchanted Rock, located 18 miles (29 kilometers) north of Fredericksburg, is the second largest outcropping of pink granite in the United States. American Indians believed spirits in the rocks groaned. The sounds they heard were actually the rock cooling after being heated by the sun.

Pecans are grown in many parts of Texas. The Texas pecan crop averages about 60 million pounds (27 million kilograms) a year.

Llano Basin

The Llano (LAN–oh) Basin is a small area of lower elevation, about 1,000–1,800 feet (305–550 meters) on the northern edge of the Edwards Plateau. It has small streams and rock outcroppings. This mineral-producing area is the only place where blue topaz, the state gemstone, is found.

The Llano Basin receives about 30 inches (76 centimeters) of rain a year. This is enough for ranching and some farming. There are no large cities in the Llano Basin. Trees of the area include mesquite and pecans. San Saba calls itself the Pecan Capital of the World. Llano calls itself the Deer Capital of Texas. Brady is within 15 miles (24 kilometers) of the exact center of Texas. Mason has many houses constructed of the red sandstone that was taken from buildings at the abandoned Fort Mason on the ridge above the town.

Mountains and Basins

The Mountains and **Basins** region is sometimes called Trans-Pecos, which means "across the Pecos River." The Mountains and Basins region is in extreme west Texas and is the driest, windiest, and least populated of all the Texas regions. The soil is sandy or rocky. Most of the land is flat, except where tall mountains rise. Summer temperatures climb high enough to be life-threatening. Monahans, about 35 miles (56 kilometers) west of Odessa, reached 120°Fahrenheit (49°Celsius) in 1994. This matched the state record set in Seymour in 1936.

Mountains and Basins Region of Texas

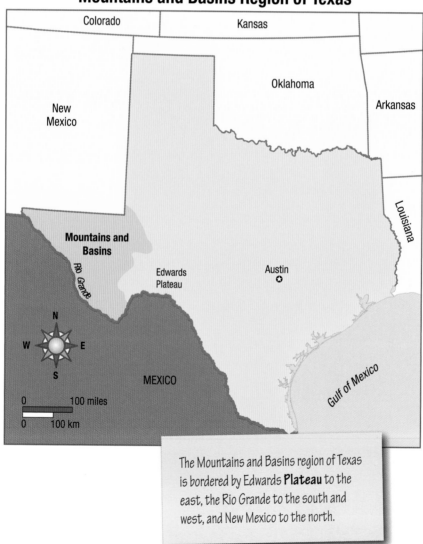

The Mountains and Basins region of Texas is bordered by Edwards **Plateau** to the east, the Rio Grande to the south and west, and New Mexico to the north.

The Mountains and Basins region is mostly known for its national parks. Guadalupe National Park on the New Mexico border contains the highest point in Texas. Guadalupe Peak reaches 8,749 feet (2,667 meters). Just south of it is *El Capitan*, which is also more than 8,000 feet (2,438 meters) high.

Pine Springs, at the top of Guadalupe Pass, is the windiest place in Texas. From February to April, winds there can average up to 80 miles per hour (129 kilometers per hour), with gusts up to 105 miles per hour (169 kilometers per hour).

Monahans Sandhills State Park

Monahans Sandhills State Park has huge sand **dunes**. American Indians knew where to dig between the dunes for water. Today, visitors enjoy sand surfing. The park also has one of the largest oak forests in the nation. The Harvard oaks are rarely over 3 feet (91 centimeters) tall.

El Capitan, which means "the Captain," is more than 8,000 feet (2,439 meters) high. It is a peak in Guadalupe National Park.

Big Bend National Park is at the tip of the big bend in the Rio Grande. The park is the size of the state of Rhode Island. The Chisos Mountains are completely within its borders. On the Rio Grande, the walls of Boquillas (bo–KEE–yus), Mariscal, and Santa Elena (SAN–tuh e–LAY–nuh) Canyons rise more than 1,600 feet (488 meters) above the river. Among the **fossils** found in the park is the largest known **pterodactyl** (TEHR–uh–dak–tul), with a wingspan of 51 feet (15.5 meters).

The Rio Grande winds its way through the limestone walls of huge canyons within Big Bend National Park in the Mountains and Basins region.

Oldest Town in Texas

On the edge of El Paso is Ysleta (is–LEHT–uh). It was founded in 1680 by Tigua (TEE–wuh) Indians fleeing from New Mexico. The Tigua **Reservation** is still there today. Ysleta is the oldest town in Texas. It used to be in Mexico, but the Rio Grande changed course, making it part of Texas.

West of Big Bend National Park, along the Rio Grande, are some interesting ghost towns. Millions of dollars worth of **cinnabar**, which contains mercury, was mined in Terlingua (ter–LING–guh) in the 1890s. Mining operations at Terlingua basically stopped when the price of mercury went down and the demand lessened after World War II (1939–1945). Without work, people moved out of Terlingua.

About 10 miles (16 kilometers) west of Terlingua is Lajitas (luh–HEE–tus). In 2001 a developer began building a luxury resort for people with enough money to fly their own planes into this isolated area. The highway that runs westward from Lajitas is called *El Camino del Rio*, which means "river road" in Spanish. It is one of the most **scenic** roads in the nation. It passes abandoned movie sets at river level. At times it climbs magnificent red cliffs 1,000 feet (305 meters) above the river.

The River Road ends at Presidio, a quiet border city. People have been farming here along the river for 10,000 years. A road continues past Presidio but stops about 50 miles (80.5 kilometers) farther upriver. To reach El Paso, motorists must go north to Marfa. The road north to Marfa passes Shafter, an abandoned silver mining town.

The River Road (*El Camino del Rio*) is seen here running next to the Rio Grande between Fort Leaton and Terlingua, Texas.

Fort Bliss is an important part of El Paso's economy. The fort was established in 1854. Today, it is the headquarters for the United States Army Air Defense Command.

Industry

Scattered among the mountains in west Texas are low areas called basins. Leading west from Guadalupe Pass to the Hueco (WHAY–ko) Mountains are salt basins on the Diablo (de–AHB–loh) plateau. The salt in the basins is thick enough to be mined and sold.

El Paso is the westernmost Texas city. It is so far west that it is in a different time zone than the rest of the state. The Spanish explorer who found the pass in 1598 called it *El Paso del Norte*, which means "the Pass of the North."

El Paso receives only about 8 inches (20 centimeters) of rain a year, which is about as much as a desert receives. However, that has not kept El Paso from becoming the fifth largest city in Texas. The city attracts **industry** because of its four ports of entry crossing the Rio Grande. *Maquiladoras* in Mexico manufacture clothing, electronics, and automotive equipment, which they then ship across the border. El Paso's large **bilingual** population attracts business offices that take customer calls from both English and Spanish speakers. Cotton farming is successful on a 75-mile (121-kilometer) stretch of the Rio Grande in this area, reaching into New Mexico.

All around Texas you can see different regions and resources that people have used to make the state what it is today. You can see eastern Texas pine forests, the treeless Panhandle, Big Bend Mountains, northern Texas prairies, southern Texas beaches, and a western Texas desert. A wide variety of places greets visitors to the state whose name simply means "friend."

Map of Texas

N
W E
S

0   100 miles
0   100 km

• Amarillo

• Tulia

Red River

Great Plains

Wichita Falls •

Central Plains

• Lubbock

Texarkana

Denton • Celina

Fort Worth • Dallas

Marshall

Stamford • • Abilene

• Waxahachie

Tyler • Sabine River

• Midland

Comanche •

Colorado River

• Waco

Lufkin •

El Paso •

Pecos •   Pecos River

• Odessa

San Angelo •

• Brady

Brazos River

• Temple

Mountains and Basins

• Mason

• College Station

Fredericksburg •
Kerrville •

✪ Austin

Beaumont •

Houston •

Del Rio •

San Antonio River

• San Antonio

Alvin •
• Galveston

Coastal Plains

Pearsall •

Rio Grande

Victoria •

Gulf of Mexico

Laredo •

• Corpus Christi

McAllen •
• Brownsville

Legend
✪   Capital
•   City
〰   River
—   State line
⌇   Region border

New Mexico | Oklahoma | Arkansas

Texas

Louisiana

MEXICO

Gulf of Mexico

Glossary

aquifer section of rock and soil that holds water

artificial made by humans

barge wide boat with a flat bottom used mainly in harbors and on rivers and canals

barrier island island near a shore that protects the shore from the effects of a large body of water

basin low, hollow area surrounded by higher land

bayou slow-running creek near the coast

bilingual able to speak two languages

bioterrorism terrorist acts that use chemicals or disease

campus grounds of a university or other school

census official count of the number of people in a place

centennial 100th anniversary

cinnabar artificial red mercury used as dye

climate weather conditions that are usual for a certain area

conservation planned management of natural resources to prevent their waste, destruction, or neglect

county seat place where county government is based

delta piece of land shaped like a triangle made by deposits of mud and sand at the mouth of a river

derrick frame or tower over an oil well for supporting machinery

distribute deliver to, spread out, or divide among several or many

diverse something made up of many different parts or kinds of things

dredge deepen and widen by scooping out and removing earth

dune hill or ridge of sand piled up by the wind

erode wash or wear away

escarpment sharp drop in the level of the land creating a cliff or steep slope

export send a good or service out of a country for profit; also the good or service that is sent out of the country

fault line crack in the earth's crust along which movement occurs

fossil remains or traces of a living thing of long ago

glacier large body of ice that moves slowly over a wide area of land

good product a person can buy

gorge narrow valley or passage with steep sides cut by a river

grain sorghum type of tall grass cultivated for grain, often used to feed livestock

Gross Domestic Product total value of the goods and services produced in a year

helium lighter-than-air gas that does not burn

high-tech short for high-technology; having to do with advanced technology and computers

industry businesses that provide certain goods or services

institution established organization

irrigate supply water to land through artificial means; irrigation refers to the act of irrigating

loam soil having the right amount of silt, clay, and sand for growing plants

maquiladora foreign-owned factory in Mexico where lower-paid workers assemble imported parts into products for export

marsh area of wet land usually overgrown with grasses and similar plants

mesquite spiny tree or shrub that often forms thickets and has sweet pods eaten by livestock

migrate move from one region to another, or pass from one region to another on a regular schedule

mission church community set up by traveling priests called missionaries

mohair fabric or yarn made from the long hair of a goat

mollusk animal that usually lives in water and has an outside shell, such as an oyster

natural resource something available from the land that can be useful to humans

outcropping rock formation sticking up through the surface of the ground

peninsula piece of land extending out into a body of water

petrochemical chemical taken from petroleum or natural gas

petroleum raw oil obtained from wells drilled in the ground

plateau broad, flat area of high land

playa round, sunken places on the High Plains

pterodactyl type of dinosaur with a beak and wings

recreation exercise or other forms of enjoyable activity; fun

reef chain of rocks or ridge of sand at or near the surface of the water

refinery place with machinery used to bring metals, oil, or sugar to a pure state

reservation land set aside by the government for American Indians

reservoir place where water is collected and stored for use; artificial lake created by a river dam

scenic having views of natural scenery

suburb city or town just outside a larger city

tectonic plate huge segment of the earth's crust that moves

temperate not too hot nor too cold

tradition belief or custom handed down from one generation to another

tributary stream flowing into a larger stream or a lake

unique one of a kind or very unusual

urban relating to the city

Find Out More

Further Reading

Shea, Theresa. *The Texas Wildfires.* New York: Rosen Publishing, 2007.

Sievert, Terri. *Texas.* Mankato, MN: Capstone Press, 2003.

Stewart, Mark. *Regions of the World: The United States and Canada.* Chicago: Heinemann Library, 2008.

Websites

http://www.tpwd.state.tx.us/kids/about_texas/regions/
This fascinating site provides information about the state's different regions.

http://www.tx.nrcs.usda.gov/
The U.S. Department of Agriculture provides this site with information and links about Texas's many different resources.

Index